Coming Out Of The Darkness!

Now I See You!

1) Now I See You!
2) When It's Time To Make , Change Will You Yes Or No?
3) What Makes Me Mad Is A World Of Unfairness.
4) When You Ask Someone For Help?
   Does It Make You Mad?
5) How Do You Know When It's Time?
   To Say Goodbye?
6) Have You Gotten Your? Replacement Orders Yet?
7) Dependent
8) Independently Living Your Life?
9) Back On Point!
10) Energy For The Wounded Warrior!
11) Pain Don't Give Up!
12) Never Forget True Love!

One of the most unreliable things about life, is reality of everything in life itself. The justifications of not having that open mind, is the road to failure. Falling in love, just saying hello to someone; can change the way you think and one instant in time. Once you able to come out into, this world full of its sunlight; life begins! This transformation of life is no different, then the outgoing and the incoming tide of the ocean. Is it true the feeling that you go through, or is it term with the thoughts that you are having? Are you the one who will sacrifice, or are you the one who will continue to stand tall? Have you been trying to successfully, or un-successively living the life that you live this day? You believe in him who has put you on this path, or you believe in many who loved; to continue to live in the world of darkness. Can you count it many times one can say, the words I love you in a day?

Can you count the many times, one will believe you really love them; no matter how many times a day you say those words??? Is there a reason that you are still where you are, and not what you want to be? A blessing comes when you know, what do blessing is really for; did you forget the reason for the blessing. Not only do horses have walked the blinders years, look around you and see all the marriages that have disappeared! Be not the one who points that finger, for many who have not taken the time; to share the problems they saw coming their way. Now I see you, even though I saw you on the screen; I was the one who kept saying it could not be? Have you ever read a roadmap pointed out the way, somehow that that at home; and gotten lost anyway. I cannot point my fingers at anyone for the troubles I see, glory hallelujah. Sometimes I'm up and sometimes I'm down.

The good thing about life, take the time to look all around. Coming out of the darkness, how many times have I said I love you; his love supposed to hurt this way! Whichever one you are you still a spouse, in love until the end; this was the words that the book said. Whether I'm right or whether I'm wrong, every time I fall in love; the winds grow strong. Is when the thunder strikes all through the night, the brains I did have blown throughout the land; still thinking of the great love we once had? Is it wrong to say I love you, when from the beginning I knew; many others were of important nests in your world then I. But you always believe that you can find a way, to make you believe with true love lasts each and every day. The support I have for you but never go away, whenever you call for help; I shall be on my way!

Now I see you and now I understand is time for me to go and walk the land. Understand it is true that I am human and anger falling out of my brains. Anger has gotten in my way of thinking, all of the roadblocks you have put in my way. A human being this is true, I still feel like a damn fool; all the love I had for you. I can be called by any name, is no different than the games that people play. There is no one to blame and is no reason to blame anyone. The only dumb one who has no brains, is me myself and I.

I can scream and I can yell, and I can holler. You who I did love it was with all my heart, this is something that no human being can never take away from me! Have you ever heard someone say, you have learned a hard way; sometimes you need a whipping sometimes you need someone to whip you? If a mother was here, I would be able to talk to her; holder my arms and cry like a baby. I have nothing to say badly about anyone, which is truly once again a waste of time. I understand in your eyes, I'm not exactly what you want; or exactly what you need. My love for you is I think you, for the little ones that are now in my future to come. Understand this father in heaven, has always pointed out the way; for there is a reason for everything.

Now I see you and this I hope you understand, the changes that will come; other changes from his hands. I am so thankful for the things that about to happen, and the blessing of the life about to begin. Coming out of the darkness is his blessing, can you see that he's pointing the way. Life changes each and every day, these are the blessings I pray all day. Have faith in him or father in heaven and have faith in thyself. You are never alone, and it does that matter where you are. The lights were shining as we began, and then the darkness came.

There are no fingers to point, this is the worst thing a human being can do; never forget that love which was there and how it disappeared? My understanding of way you want to be, if not the same place as me. This reward that you will be happy to have, will soon be put right in your hands. But I am a soldier in my father's Army and will walk all day long; in and out of every battle in life. My apologies to you as I walk away, hoping will still be friends at the end of the day. Now I see you and I knew that soon it would end, was such powerful friends; it has always pointed to the end. One can never come between two friends; the end would come sooner; then the time that we spent this day. To all of the spouse's women/men, love each other as a family; be careful who you let enter in. Coming out of the darkness, now I see you and now I don't.

When It's Time To Make A Change Will You.

Yes Or No?

Are you one saying the words, what the hell is he talking about now? This is not the first time in your life, that things have entered into what you call a brain; and you had to take time to stop and think. Intelligent is what many like to talk with you, only because they believe this is who you are. But intelligence only comes from the level, and a fortitude in which that level of your brain is on.

Has there ever been a time in your life and you said to yourself; where in the hell did that come from. Have you heard the phrase a lesson, can be learned in more the one way? No is not the language in which we speak, but the knowledge in which we seek. Once you can travel out amongst the land, understand the reason that you on this trip. Nor the latitude or the altitude, must never stand in your way; it could be the best thing that happened when you're on your way. When it's time to make a change, will you yes or no? Or will you live under the same umbrella, when not a damn thing to show. No one said it would be easy, for you to have an outstanding and wonderful day. Is when you at that point in time, I know there's a different destination deep in your mind. I have stayed where I am put countless years, not want to leave because of the endless fears. The process of elimination will happen very quick, what you get your head out of your ass; and go on your first trip. You and not here for discomfort will make someone feel despair, is when you get tired that you'll have to disappear.

If you need that reason that we have all been looking for, I hope you stop and listen to what I'm about to say. That door has always been in front of you, open it and then walk away. To feel unjustified and more than 1000 ways, look up at the sunlight and feel is outstanding raise. You are not the only one who lived through hell this way, once you open your mind you feel a better way. Yes, talk is cheap, and many would not understand what was just said. I myself have felt this way and here I laid in the same bed every day. The starting of this journey first you must understand, don't you they appoint or blame anyone in any way. The weight that comes upon us can be heavy as hell at times, the only fault I know because I had no open mind. Education is one thing and intelligence is two things. Never forget an open mind unlocks the door in any way. Whatever the case you may have been in, those days are now at an end. Why are you still there and why are things still not clear? The number one reason is because, you were still sitting there. We all understand those sayings. You can lead a horse to water, but you cannot make it drink. On the intelligence side, nor can you make it think; but the same damn reason there's no way for you to leave. Your life is not that much different, then the person you're angry at; who makes you feel so bad. 99.5 of every human being, never takes the time to think of changing everything. Consequences can be good as well as they can be bad. Would you know any difference, if you never gave a damn? When it's time to make the change, only you can say yes and only you can say no.

It is not the time or how long to make the change, if you learn to use your brain. Diagnostics it is not a big word, it's about finding your way in life. An open mind works in many ways, when you hear and listen to what people say. People want to conquer one must understand, what it will take to conquer this land. Raise your right hand if you understand, the words yes and no. No, I don't care for that you will say at times and yes I love those colors is when you learn to draw the line. This is not my first time stepping out to get relief, if not the amount of times I've hoped it never happens again to me. Here I am as I walk this land with some, of the problems I may never understand. Stop thinking of yourself of being misunderstood, if you know what I know you have been gone and lived in the woods. Many don't see you as a good person, which is separated from where you all. It's you who must never forget, you are a shining star. I still remember the TV box with the TV on top, and the blanket on the floor.

This is how I started out once before, if my mind is open; this is one of the main reasons you hear me say to words. Help is on the way! Of course, you for down and yes you get up. Stop and think of others with problems in the same way, it will wonder why you see them out and about the next day. I am one who sees the future and of course many of you still don't understand. For whatever reason, is he wants me to walk this land? Things do change this you must understand, but first you must get up out of the chair. As our veterans always say. Here today gone tomorrow, in other words do it while you're here; course you may not be here tomorrow. When it's time to make a change, where you yes or no. I'll keep living in hell, knowing no one is going to show. Someone looks at you as the bad guy or bad girl, this you already know. Therefore, get up and start a brand-new show, which many ways of making you smile will show up; then and only then will you take the time to grow up. This is not for you who have no problems and live in such a graceful way. But will you yes or no, it's bound to come your way! With his blessing from heaven I am happy these words of wisdom will be near, just in case family down, the tears. Wendy is a broken heart for any reason, I hope you know it makes no difference what season. Don't get mad as they say get glad, there's always a way to be better in ways to make you smile, when you walk out the door leave everything on the floor. If you are happy-go-lucky and had that outstanding smile than it is here is for you for you to reconcile. Help is on the way understand the words that I say. When it's time to make a change, will you yes or no???

What Makes Me Mad Is.

A World Of Unfairness.

I would like to start this chapter, by saying something a little different; that is in difference to other chapters. Each one of us remembers some things deep in our minds from our past. One of the things that I remember, and I am still associate with doing. Is enjoying a peanut butter and strawberry jelly sandwich. From a baby there are things I remember, knowing this point of times 70 years later; I am steals eating peanut butter and strawberry sandwiches. I don't weigh as much as I used to as a small boy and I've lost 26 pounds. It is for the first time in 40 something years I weigh in at 212 pounds. This is one outstanding excellent point, in my life today. My last drink of alcohol of any kind, was in Puerto Rico and this took place before the belt told; for the New Year's in Puerto Rico at 12 o'clock. What is hard for many to understand, is saying to people that be in a human computer; can be one hell of a way of life.

What goes in and what comes out is hard for those to understand, because it's the results that the actions of why a certain event went on. When one analyzes the world of alcoholism, especially when one has not had a drink of water; and the last 10 years. Being told how to solve the problem only comes with results, of the information one has time to enter in. The most horrific thing in life is understanding thyself, forging your mind to say this is totally not me. For one to tell me that I will stop drinking, is outrageously impossible and embarrassing to me to find a better way of life's sober. Whomever it may be in authority high above in the sky, or somewhere load deep in the trances of darkness. Can only be a total waste of their time, ensuring me of a better way of life. Number one worm comes from understanding or ways of life, ABC, makes no difference to me; one the analyzation's come forth to be positive and far from negative. It was my timeline of duels and don'ts plus analyzing if this was for me. There was no way in hell I was ever thinking of not drinking, then along came the spider that sat down beside her. Where one may think it's a joke other can survive, by taking the steps needed to survive. I am being sober your talk with the person, this was my life and I love living in this way! Do you still remember the peanut butter and strawberry jelly sandwich?

If it was good for you then and you still eat net now is what we learn all pass and are present and our future can change for the better. Laugh if you want of how I live my life, you have no way of knowing of all my sacrifice. Of all the things I have been told that you cannot do, all who told me this turn into fools. Of all the things that you want to put four, yes, we can show the world our father in heaven is the boss. When it is that you have faith in him is when your life shall begin, on your way up from falling; take the time to look all around. I still remember the day that I was not looking where I was walking, I hit that poll fell so cold. The first thing I did was looked all around I was hoping no one has seen, this alcoholic hit that ground. With a smile on my face I got up walked away from that place, in my mind I said that was a damn shame. Lo and behold you thought you got away with murder, until somebody said I saw you fall like a hamburger.

People don't pay attention to the worth of the said, big brothers always watching you. The words I just said keep them in your head, someone always sees everything that happens to you and to me! For me not to drink alcohol had to be one hell of a trip, you mean I can have a drink on the night of St. Nick. They sent me away I was over 135 days and all I've ever heard were about those who fell started all over again. You all know I'm sick, but he is the trick, and his computer I will analyze it.

Things like me to be where something is wrong with a guy fit nobody in that chair, what the brain let his that never quits will come to life is he living. If you think I am the only one don't be no fool, I met 10 or 11 right there in school. The things I have been asked to do, but only blow your mind; being with a mind like mine all I did was analyze. The professor said I send everyone to your house, one that day for the college they can log in and then log out. Can you tell my neighbors why there was a line outside my door, even though I lived up on the fourth floor? It does not make it different what you ask me to do, the bed understand I will analyze you to. Being an alcoholic and drug addict that I was, a better way of living was on my list from above.

God our father in heaven I love him so much, all the things that he asked me keeps my mind; in that world that I love. Don't think for a moment that you could do this alone, the person that he gave me blow my mind were rocks and stones. Passes onto somebody that you know and tell them the words being said I'm not from a TV show. My sponsor will someone who blew my mind, then I had to go back and find my mind wherever it was in time. 135 days clean and sober I analyze this time and I thought it was a crime. When I went away to get clean and sober, I was called a book worm, who would analyze and read everything on sobriety.

The first week I was there I ate very little food, and this stop me from doing that to. Once again, I was in a place called humans and people would different in so many ways. On my last day of being there sobriety, many was saying goodbye. It was my turn and they said this bookworm was not going to survive. I changed the way I ate and also change the way I was thinking of how to become sober. When they signed my paperwork, the group said I would be back, there is no way in hell I can become clean and sober reading up on the facts. Hearing so many times of how many had to come back, because they had lived in full back into the alcohol. This is not for you to become clean and sober or to become drug-free. This is someone telling the story, of how what happened to me. 135 days clean and sober and in Puerto Rico I was the only one with my friends and family who was not drinking. I love how they honored my sobriety, with respect honor and Justice. It was when the countdown started, five, four, three, two, one. That I looked over and saw that can of beer. I reached down and I picked up that can of beer, and I took a quick swallow. It was when I turned around to look at all my family members, in Puerto Rico the room was silent. My girlfriend at that time said you would do only one sober here, boy what a fool. There was no happy New Year's there was no clapping and there was no yelling. I believe I spoiled did they even though there was no intention of doing so to anyone.

When I looked at her, I picked up my cell phone, and called my sponsor. I told him what I had just done, and my sponsor said to me these words; that I remember to this day! My sponsor said to me why dad is great now every New Year's Day, you'll be clean and sober each day. I said you mean every New Year's Day I can't take a drink, he said to me Johnnie what the hell do you think. Being as hotheaded as I am in more than one way, I am told don't you know it is God who moves in mysterious ways! If you family were to tell me that one day at a time, January 1, 2020 12:01 AM. Johnnie H. Williams Jr. will be 30 years clean and sober. Even I would never believe that, but the facts of the human computer; is from 19 12:01 AM – 2024 1 AM = 30 years clean and sober. Family can you see the same thing that I feel about the peanut butter and strawberry jelly sandwich. That I have been eating all my life, it's healthy and good for me. If you have not read any of my books, then not about the money. They are all out you and how intelligent that you are. If not when you take the fall, is when you get up and look around get up and be proud that you not still on that ground. Intelligence come from the inside and the outside, do you have to look to the left or to the right to see what's going down. When people talk to you take the time to listen, I analyze every word you said in which I can live a better life this day. Hold your hand out and pull somebody up, I don't remember then name or who they were. But I do know it was an angel from above! What makes me mad is just whirl of unfairness, and till I take the time and move on without all of the said sadness!

When You Ask Someone For Help.

Does It Make You Mad?

I have an organization by the name of. Help Is On The Way For Veterans 1024 CORP. One of the reasons I came up with this name, was to provide help for veterans and all families. It would not make sense, for me to tell you how many times; that I have asked someone to help. What you yourself and I must understand is the leadership ability that we need. The word help comes in many shapes and forms, possibly make you think that that train has showed up. The power of the brain most people do not understand, how you use it will open the door. Leadership you must learn, with the possibility of getting a ass whipping. When you calculate the word ass whipping, it depends upon it be in a good or a bad thing, which you needed from the very start.

Understand the language in which I use, because the words are in the Bible; they not of me as a bad person with a big mouth. Nor ox or ass is in the Bible, with ways of asking for help also that is needed. I can tell you of the office in which I received, that led me to believe I will be a rich man; not a poor man.
Leadership you think of as educational, therefore this is at the top of my list. When you do graduate and find yourself on the way up. Many times, you find yourself falling, the nationally and provocation of you thinking of bettering your life. Is the thinking of many in leadership, that have led you to the point in time; that I am now ready to move forward in life. In return of your reality, you end up with two jobs and still not enough to pay your rent. Your put upon the path in which your now are asking for help. Your anger is now starting to

show, in possibility of you think in this way; now you are finding yourself or your days and still pray for a better day. Help is what you have asked for, how can this be so hard. You did take the time to climb that ladder, there was this sign in front of you; that said leadership step this way. Could the possibility of my thinking, lead be down the wrong path? Why is it that you have reached this point in time, in which I don't want to live my life this way? I myself have asked for help and take the time to make sure you live a better way.

My way of thinking is to help each person, to live a better way! is not easy for me to pay my bills every day. They are so many promises that others will make you, what really hurts is how it is totally untrue. I talk with many people each day, and everyone says the words help is on the way. Life is not easy and how we live it many unhappy with how their life is this day. I had a conversation with a friend of mine, she was mad and angry how things worked out this day. The young ladies' words were my daughter works two jobs and cannot find an apartment. We have asked for help and can't find any till this day. Many have said will call you back, for whatever reason this never happened. I have talked to people who wanted to move forward in life, many said we are here to help you; this turned out to be a lie. With all the leadership's abilities, that led you to this time and place; what makes you mad is the people in front of your face. When you graduate you have nothing to worry about, your job will be in place. When you appeared with all your tears, because there is no help in any way. I have been there, and I have done that. You are a leader, and everything is in place. I ended up doing my own copyright once I may call, I found the way. I needed help and I could not find it, I open my mind and found a better way. Does it make you mad and doesn't make you said when you walk throughout this land? In the world of leadership is not one day you will stop in order to learn.

How to get up off that ass and make that right turn. I ended up in Central Park, way I sat down and made at least 10 other calls on my cell phone. Also, the people I set out to see this day, said no we don't do things that way. I have prepared myself to go down and talk with them. On that path everyone I stopped to see; said they could not help me. I have studied and prepared myself for that day, but I was not prepared for the words those people would say. It was your leadership abilities, that put you on that path. It has been a long time since I sat in Central Park, then I look at all the people going to and frog that I said it's time for me to go home. As a leader this fight is not the end, here I was in the Bronx library educating myself with some friends. I found a place to sit and talk to use the computers again. That's when I found out the secret, and my copyrights program began. I now have two books copyrighted and I am the owner not my friends. With your leadership you are a leader, and no way in hell will that ever end. This was one hell of a trip and I was in the ups and downs with no help to be found. Does it make you mad, or does it make you sad; I felt lonely with no one to talk to. I understand people telling you, we are here to keep it help you need. Of all the eight places I went, the information tells what they do; until they are standing right in front of you. No, I won't tell a name and yes to me it is a game of all the publicity out there that is to blame. Do you have an appointment sir is what I was asked, I made my way all the way down there; but no one told me I needed a pass.

Asking for help and being angry at the same time, will not help you to move any faster in time. Sometimes we must take a moment and bring ourselves together. In that moment of time you can also called a friend, that's where the conversation begins. Your leadership abilities can only set in, when things are not working right; are you a leader who can step in? We are invincible what the things we can do, is how you stand up; don't be the person looking for the end. There was total hell of me asking for help till this day, when I picked up the phone at that point in time I was on my way. Did you call the copyright people and what I did, and I found out made a better day?

My previous for other books, I am thankful for the blessing of this day. What the copyright people told me; I now can do a better way. You believe that you are here to learn something, and then the years pass away. Is not to you make that phone call, that you find out you always a better way. If it was not for my anger sitting there in Central Park, then led me to the library back home in the Bronx. Being a leader walking on that path, open your eyes and clean out your ears.

Before you know what, a joy will appear, at a make you happy by your way thinking has now made our day. It would be lovely every time someone said I'm here to help you, if it was true. I should be one of the richest people, what they beautiful smile upon my face. When you're on the path one must understand, if you call yourself a leader you must walk across the land. Of course, is not going to be easy and hell yes you will be upset. Never forget while you're out there, that you will learn from the best. They advertise how they can help me, and I made my trip down that way; it reminds me of many others in my path will have not helped me till this day. Yes, there are many who can help you along your way, whole your head up high and enjoy your day. You will be called yourself a leader and now understand the words that I say. I hope and pray that you can help someone and make it a better day. If you think for one moment that this will stop in time, ask someone to help you; then pick up the napkin and wipe your eyes. What happened to you also happens to others, as a leader your decisions are because you are that leader. With that open mind you know you have to run the costs, that is to be the boss. Therefore, if you are the boss, you will have to pay the course.

The three days that I walked in my brain fell out my head, I ended up writing another book instead. The things that you do, will help you get through. Have faith in thyself and what it is that you plan to do, say a prayer because he's always there with you. You can always ask for help; this I constantly do. It does not mean the hell you asked for, someone will walk you through. All I had to do was pick up the phone, and all I had to do was make the call. To the copyright people, not to the others then led me along. Always think positive in life for all the things you do, with that open mind you will get through it to. Be blessed, like all the rest. My organization Help Is On The Way For Veterans 1024 CORP. I am there to provide the help that is needed, as if I were to one asking for help. Being a leader, keeps me on my way. God bless and have a great day! Johnnie H. Williams Jr. Vietnam Combat Veteran 199th Light INF. 4/12 (TET 1968).

How Do You Know When It's Time?

To Say Goodbye?

When they won't even say good morning to you and you still trying your best to be a human being. One of the most amazing accuracies about life, is when one becomes a productive human computer; in which many things that resonate through their minds are accurate and to the point. Naturally fomenting the mind can only work certain phases, the termination/fact abilities/full control of the possibilities of information going in and coming out.

Dedication to get yourself out of the situations in which you know find yourself in, a basically you are getting your head out of your ass!!! Understanding the input is one thing, analyzing the output is another. When they don't talk to you, but when their cell phone/home phone rings there is total and enjoyment in the conversations at hand. The immoralities of life, other factors of realities. Many do not understand the words just said, but taking the time to analyze; *your life from the outside looking in. As in many times stated before there is a reason for everything, in which you must look to your right and to your left. Transformations can only be performed, in two different ways; the fascinations are the outcome of which you put in. Many times, have you waiting for the results, of the report all about you? Were the presentations accurate or the words misspelled, the implications and accuracies point the way to you. Stop for one moment and think for yourself, is this about me. One day or 25 years, is a better or is it worse. Are you thinking as one, or thinking without each other?*

Is that reason why you are still there, because deep in your heart you really care. We already said we do not point fingers, nor do we play the blame game. Is there a reason why you listen to what I'm saying, do you feel this is happening to you? Did you just say oh my God he's thinking the same way I do?   Don't take the time to think bad of others, when you can change the way that you are; with your brain you can go far. Are you sitting their thinking, which way do I get the hell out of here? Were you the one who put yourself where you are, sitting their looking at yourself dreaming of how I can go far; to a better place where there is a beautiful Lake and Mountains and deer's all over the place? Hate that gray don't wash it away, get up and find yourself a better way. How do you know when it's time to say goodbye, when they walk right past you; as if you're not even alive. So many of you think this might be a joke, I am not the only one who feels this way. Can you say to them I love you and they looked all the other way; why in the hell am I still sitting on this couch today! I never talk about the money, because it always gets in the way; now do you understand why I am broke today. How many bills I pay and continue to live this way. My money is your money and your money is your money. How many just understood, the words I just said. Yes, we are all family these all the words I say, what I don't understand your words come out a different way?

Why would someone say I love you, when the words mean nothing on this day? It's when you take the time to put the project together, the outcome of the project; should be amazingly accurate in every way. Your dedication and your accuracy/performance must be formatted in a special way. Once you see through the years, the accomplishments and dedication all falling apart. It is your conclusion what must be done, to stay or depart. Amazing how many things I need to get through this mess, they can give a damn you're no longer the best. The advantage of the accuracy of your brain, what the hell is wrong; what you don't feel the pain! It is you who is the fool who was being overruled, it is your brain that is not the same; take the time to put in a new battery in today.

Don't feel ashamed that there's no accuracy in your brain, your way of thinking every day is shrinking. Instead of all the time saying the words yes, what the hell happened to the word no. I'm not going to do this anymore, now go and pick your brains up off the floor. If no love/sex/kissing/hugs/smiles for months at a time. If no love therefore who needs the money, when there is no honey. You may think I'm the only one thinking this way, think of the other half as they go out to play.

Do you feel alone and sorry that you are alone and by yourself? Do you feel that others may see the separation, between you and between me? As usual your friends have first place, I can't even remember our last date. When you go and you come home! You own the words that one can say, this is your house! This is your home and it will only run one way! The same way it is run each and every day! I'm not mad and I am not angry because things are about to change. I'm going to hold my head high and thank God as I look into the sky. I will keep thinking of my motto. Help is on the way! I will not be here long, how do you know when it's time to say goodbye? It was my father in heaven who said the words, Johnnie you still alive!!! By the time you are reading this book I pray and hope you understand, Johnnie H. Williams Jr. Is back out walk the land!

Have You Gotten Your?

Replacement Orders Yet?

   You may in this time of your life be wondering, why am I still have here. At the top of the list there is no money and the bill still have to be paid. You can always enjoy someone talking about you, like the dog many at this time probably think you. I understand civilians may not know what I'm talking about, when the questions asked; have you got your replacement orders yet. These are the orders Uncle Sam gives to you, which say you're moving to a new location.

A reading the books that I write, there are no lies or ways to talk of others; that will make you feel that you are not the one who you say you are. You the reader will not tell others; of all the dilemmas you go through every day in life. I work for my father in heaven, and the words which you read our true. You would never alone and many of you never look up. When you think he is not there, our father in heaven is always near. If you think I'm the only one living in hell, you are so wrong only because you have not been in that storm! I'm making coffee every morning for 20 something years and to be told this morning August 18, 2019.

Don't make my coffee! With a statement like that there is nothing for one to say, you are the one who must get out and enjoyed this day. No, you are not point in the finger and all of you who do not understand; it will never be a better way of life for you. Until this day I have been sleeping on the couch, for the last 12 to 14 days and it doesn't make sense to keep account when you're the one still sleeping on the couch!   Many think you should get up get the hell out, but you dear move out until all those problems have been put out. Intelligent is what one can always be, when you open your eyes and see what I see. Yes, they will still talk about you like a dog, this will be okay because you won't be there for long.

   Before you leave say a prayer with me, even in my case I can't get down off of my feet. Do not put the blame on anyone but yourself, this way when you leave if no guiltiness in the house.   Good morning all words many say each and every day. Not when there's nothing to talk about, they walk right past you anyway. You can walk pass a human being, that you do not know in any way, that person or pass you and say to words have a wonderful day. Are you at home walking around like you're all alone, what they coming in or the day going out; it makes no difference you still sitting on the couch? Yes, I have my replacement orders, the words that you say get your head out your ass; then leave the proper way. Do not run out the door then act like the other jerk, who ended up in jail for the words that were said because he was mad as that jerk. Thank you, father, for this day and everything in it, all the words I say. Angry, mad, confused, PTSD, state of how away from me! The only thing you are doing, is preparing me to live alone. I cook and clean and know how to care for myself. So, will be in October 24, 2019, I will be 71 years young. The wilderness is what I love, thanks to my father from above; wherever he sent to me they can only be pure love. Even my world of credit scores has fell so far in hell and his stupidest of me kicking ass has kept me out of hell.

In the last two months I called to find out, if I can get help with book number five; suicide stop it now and book number six who am I! As I spoke to the young man, he told me yesterday, also three weeks ago but the SBA; who said they couldn't help me? The biggest problem is we never read between the lines, because way on the couch still crying. The young man was so nice that I finally took the time, to understand the words he was saying. Johnnie we cannot help you with the biggest credit that is bad, is of you owning $675 to a bank in New York City. This is the most you all anybody, in the world today. Once again, I said to myself what a dummy who has worked so hard to clean up his credit and everything is just about done at this day and time. Family understand what I'm trying to tell you, being angry, frustrated, bandwidth thinking and led down the wrong path. Because we do not take the time, to continue on to make things fine. Are you sitting on the couch or sleeping on one side of the bed; are you walking around like the dead. Do you think the reasons dear no kisses and hugs, as many say no love? Standing tall will help you get through it all, you're the one who knows your case and you the one who knows your faith. This is not to take the time to talk bad about others, you the one who is not sleeping good on the need that cover.

Tomorrow's another day is what many people say, when you get your replacement orders only then do you go out and play. Is there a clean bill of health and the way that you separate? You will be happy to know, and Uncle Sam says the words, drop and give me 50. With few new credit score and your new apartments, which will lead the way to your new two-family home. Hell, no you will not be all alone, he is looking down and sees not a frown on your face; it was you kept your faith. Here today and gone tomorrow is what our veterans say, do me a small favor and get the hell out of my way. Yes, you could be angry also yes you could be mad, what the hell is that good for to the dummy does still sitting there. If you think for one minute that I am not angry and that I am not mad? I think the opposite for my ass ends up in jail and that was because I don't do that anymore. You human beings are just as human as I am. PTSD once again is my world and I see it coming therefore I teach it who is the boss. I go to the gym for my workout, still have heart attacks, still have strokes and with the hell does that mean. Not a damn thing! Here today and gone tomorrow and no stop sign with your name is how many will remember who you were. But the good thing is that love and kindness you shared while you were here. Family you must get on the path, this is also inside of the Bible and the path shows you the way each and every day. Are you still sitting on a couch when hell you want to get up and get out? Don't be no dummy and no you have no money, never forget help is on the way each and every day. Take your time before you go out to play, make sure everything is ready for you so you can stand up and say to words. Help is on the way!!!

Dependent?

Independently Living Your Life?

How many of you are willing to raise your right hand, and say that you are dependent on someone? Are you a female or male who has worked all your life, finding yourself a person who must depend; on someone to care for you. The only different categories of what is called dependent, in which the topic can be what you are dependent on. Can it be your one who is finding how hard it is, just to think of having someone that you must depend upon; to be there and point the way in your life. One it is in your point in time in your life, that you are depending on someone to make up your bed, to help put on your clothing; to feed you each and every day. Being one who was depending is not easy when you are the dependent. In the world of be in a dependent person, looking and needing help this you must understand.

Dependent on what stage you may be in, at this time in your life. You must plan and stay wide awake for all things in your life. Being dependent does not have to be bad, the word dependent shows you that you need help. On the other hand, if you are independently living your life, where you are the one who still can stand up and say yes or no to how things go. Then you must be the one in charge of the things in your life, we're off you are not doing it by yourself and many others are there to help and give that helping hand. Pretty soon I will be back in the world of independently living at that date and time all the choices will be mine.

Know this is not my first time on this trip, independency and moving forward in life. No way in hell this is going to be easy, without family nearby some can make it and some cannot. Never forget the loneliness that will set in when you're living independently, only when you find time to offset the sadness will be gladness. One who is a dependent does not have to depend on so many things. One who is living independently is the one who runs the show. Your ups and your downs don't forget your ends and yet out. Can help you to fall down. If the plans that you make that many call the mistake, get up off the floor and put a smile on your face.

I thank my father in heaven for this day and everything in it, all my prayers each and every day. I am a dependent person in life and understands the rules of life. Keep the faith are words I say, so you can come out for another day. S We had the daytime and, we have the nighttime, which overflows in life you must still get up and go. Whether it's the night shift or whether it is the day shift. You must get up and go out and make your world a better world to live. The good times in life can also turn into bedtimes in life, you find yourself on the trail that many have never traveled on. This is not my first tour of duty; this is my third time down the road; making sure I do not point the finger at anyone. To fall with all the garbage in your pockets, are a fact of why you can't get up. Point taken walking around and all that bad air, now you will smell what is called the fresh air. I've been down to hell and each time have come out of hell. Hell is only an educational place for me, way off I learned not to make the same mistakes again.

Why would anyone use the words, mistakes and how can one benefit from their mistakes? This will only happen once you realize, the mistakes on your own; not someone else's. It is only when we realize the roadblocks and our life, will put they're for the inconvenience of learning not to do this again. Being independent makes you the lone Wolf, in my case a scorpion looking to sustain anyone. Even one person who may be in this mode, must know when that moment comes if it is true or false. Independently can be an outstanding life, if you understand; you're the one with the sacrifice. I've been happy to be living for many years, once again they came those tears. Yes, I have been dependent on many things, for the last few years. Now putting things in order, there is no fear. If you read my books you can truly understand, on one damn veteran who has walked all throughout this land. My anger and my band this have always gotten in my way, I also know how when the time comes to live a better way. If you do not understand these words I say, you're wasting your time put this book away. Understand the love I share and how I've walked throughout the land.

I said the words I love you in my heart beats stronger each day. The only thing that hurts, is when there is no longer any love on the display. As I'm talking to you about being dependent, how does it make you feel. I've been sleeping on the same couch for 12 or 14 days, is this what you call independently living your life. Don't get mad as I am be glad, soon I will be walking out of the door; because of my heart is no love anymore. Dependent on someone to love no, dependent on someone to hold your hand no; dependent to walk with me throughout this land no. To not point the finger is set only whole your down, therefore every time we see you it's with the same frown. It makes no difference who you are, because if you feel the same way; there's always a better way. I understand why you don't love me; I understand why you don't give a damn; I'm only wanting to thank you for helping me walk back throughout the land. Do you know what happens, when you back on point?

Back On Point!

In case you didn't know why we say to words back home point, this is when you're on the frontline. One a veteran is on the frontline; this is where many of us learned the words to me: here today gone tomorrow. One else and whether Vietnam, 1968 (TET). Everyone was on the frontline, meaning this is the battlefield. Everyone had a nickname; my nickname was the lawnmower. When I first got the Vietnam, I was told that you should not make friends. This reason I learned at the first day was there, those who you said hello to; you never sought to say goodbye. It turned into a life of he or she did not make it back. There wasn't a reason to ask why, not the time to wonder when and what day did it happen. When a veteran is on point, there is nothing that veteran does not see, smell, taste, or hear. A person who has went from a severe, to a veteran will never be the same. Being on point pushed me back out in the woods, there many like myself who love it. Being on point when a decision must be made, if you have to think about that decision your dead! Being on point you said to yourself why I am broke, the time taken to ask the question and the analyzation of that question; is now done. When the commander says this is your new location, the time taken for you to analyze from top to bottom, this new location and synchronize all needed to survive.

On point you are the first one out, many calls us a scout. Your new requisition papers, plus the Compass put in your hand; get the hell up and look at that land. Your inquisitiveness to think and wonder of where we can be, sounds like you a bigger fool than me. When you're on your way out, of location number one; prepare yourself in advance for all the things that you will find there.

I hope you not sitting on a couch as I am, looking down through the valleys; for the preparation of walking with no doubt of location number two what they will be waiting for you. When the commander says to you have another week and then you through, but you didn't know is that the commander is counting on you. The person in charge understand the changes you're going to throw, but you have to get off at that thing and moved to location number two. Being one who scored from a to B to C to the. All must be in order before you go out on this day, you may not want to come back this way. I love my Uncle Sam; from him I have learned to walk in any land. I came home all alone with pain, anger, sadness, unforgiving nests. It is now called pulse traumatic stress disorder, short for PTSD. You can never take the soldier out of me, only because I am one who is already 29 hours per day. Being back on point I have learned, stop letting others know of the games that they like to play. Why am I broke what the brain that was given, because of all the dumb roadblocks and people I trust with faith. I have put together so many reasons, for veterans to take that hill, but talk is cheap and trying to work with others; sometimes is not a good idea. Back on point plus taken the time, to ask for donations in order to keep helping veterans.

 This has been a no and we love what you do not stop. When you're on point you must be able to make that decision, many in Vietnam took the time to think. Even in this life today I will be in attack mode, solely because I am out there on point. I talk with hundreds of thousands of veterans and I tell them this. You are on the frontline; you are on point only believe waste your eyes and your ears tell you. On the front lines and do not report to the rear, this is why there is never no fear. As the commander says there is no point in thinking that you're not going to the frontline. That is your destination with your estimate time of arrival on. There is no such thing of you be in late, not for the commander date. Back one point allows each discount and to look around to see if the glass is going. If you don't think that I know who you are, this is not true solely because on the way down; I will pass your stomping grounds. As a veteran who has had many a mission near and far, I love doing things and walking to the stars. I understand separation from thee, is not the separation from he; my father in heaven. No matter who you are and no matter how far your destination could be. Get up and move out, then see when life shall bring. Leave the baggage at home always walk with that open mind; things will get better in a glass of wine.

Sometimes the things happen to you and they happened to me, what the hell are you going to do; in order to live a better life is for me and it's for you. You will find yourself in places you don't want to be, one thing about that place you thought it was your destiny. I can never be taken the thoughts that are in my mind, if I had the financing I be on the other side. You may not understand that is not all about you, when you stop and think this is the only time you will go free. Some people say put eggs in one basket, then what happens is there's no basket. Have to things that were this house, I have already moved my; in the cubicle what is stacked up in an outstanding way. Many years have tried my best and now I want to protest. The best way to do something is the right way, and the only way is the best way. I hope by the time you read this book, and you say to words help is on the way. I will tell you my father in heaven, has helped me move away. Back one point keeps my mind sharp, get no time for crying and is no time for die. Get up Johnnie H. Williams Jr. and start your day!!!

Energy For The Wounded Warrior!

Once a warrior, always a warrior. You sometimes hear the expression; a mind is a terrible thing to waste. It is true having a mind and point the way to success, but only if you on the path of understanding life. The fulfillment that a put forth in front of us, and the emptiness of them not coming true; other burdens which are left upon us. Human beings prosper in so many ways, is when you turn the page you find how many stuck in the same or hold. We have so many expressions in life, one who to see and hear every day; is sorry not a winner.

How about life is a beach and don't forget about I've fallen, and I can't get up. Can you comprehend the words that are being said to you or is it that you brain so on backwards; like 85% of those walking the earth. How can I possibly know that they are 85% people, who don't know which way is up? Drugs alcohol smoking madness and the ending of life. These are the things put upon us known as roadblocks, in the essence who the hell gets a damn; I love to smoke, and I love to do drugs. This is deep in the mind of many human beings, wherefore for you listen to the words I say; I love to drink. In this sentence after that will be but being honest with myself; I do not have to drink. Having an understanding this was the words being said, comprehending the understanding this of the words being said; can only move you forward in life. When it was my turn to get clean and sober, they laughed at me. What was that I did not know, and said they were waiting for me to show up once again, not bringing others to them as I did; but me understanding why they were laughing at me.

I am still alcoholic to this day and knowing this keeps me on the path of AA. Remember the phrase God works in mysterious ways; can you understand what I'm about to say; here is another reason I say to words help is on the way. I was working on my job and they call my boss and said we going to send him away. My boss said to them one not another day, we need his hard work in here today. This is one they were talking and explain to him don't even think about it. They were his bosses standing tall over him, when I didn't know or understand will soon be the best of friends. I was told to go home, and the collar pick me up and take me to the airport. I destination was still in Virginia and there I will get clean and sober. I got a phone call and the person said come downstairs I'm here. I looked around and did not see anyone, then there was someone blowing a horn. Right in front of me was a black limousine no way in hell was this call for me. The man inside said I'm here to take you to the airport, going to get a six pack of beer; those are the words that I heard him say. Into the bodega I went and a six pack of beer I came out with. I drink this six pack all the way to the airport and I enjoyed this wonderful quiet ride. In the airport there was a long line and a short line. I got in the short line and the gentleman said. This is the VIP line and you cannot get in this line. I said to the gentleman I'm so sorry, I'm on my way to get clean and sober to live life a better way.

The gentleman said what did you say, excuse me sir go right ahead and walk this way. I do know what the reason was, but I moved on to the airplane. As I was sitting on the airplane and the airplane took off. A young lady was serving alcohol and I told her I was going to get clean and sober. She left the alcohol caught right by my side and I drank all the way to Salem Virginia. Once I departed the airplane there was a man standing, they would assign, and it had my name on it next to a bar. I won't pass the man and started to enter into the bar, that's when the man said to me, you're not even go on to walk that far. I was told and to this day still don't understand, how that man damn near took me by my hand. There was this three-hour ride, which is to our destination, the conversation in that call was truly a blessing. I went to the ins and outs plus the ups and downs. When I was about to leave to come home, I was told you nothing but a damn book or you have read everything, and you understood everything. And pretty soon you want to take another drink, because with that mighty yours you do not think; you just read books about getting clean and sober we don't think you really understand the lesson plan. While I was in AA, I kept hearing about everyone who fell, some has six years; many had 25 years and then they fell and return to drinking. Be in the book one that I am is no way in hell I'm going to wait till I fall; with the hundred and 45 days clean and sober. New Year's night and then count was 5,4,3,2,1 happy New Year's. I picked up that can of beer and took a sip therefore when others looked at me. The words that were said how stupid are you, to do what you just did. I called up my sponsor and told him what was just done, he says so in Puerto Rico you've had a lot of fun.

I was told by him did you know what you have just done, AV New Year's Day you will be sober and having fun. God works in mysterious ways; it was him who made me take that drink; it was him they said let me show you how to think. That was the year 1990 and if you know how to do the math. It means that in the year 1920, 12:01 PM I will have 30 years clean and sober; one day at a time.   Energy of a warm the warrior; is the ends and out of life. One of the problems we have especially with suicide, we don't talk or tell the people the problems at hand. There are things that happened to me that I talk about and they are the same things that happened to you that you do not talk. This is why I always say you the reader, understanding that we are both in the same boat. Energy of the wonder warrior, how many of you know how much or how many times you have been in hell. I was in basic training a young man from Bronx New York. You would think that I would understand, the shootings in the city that I grew up around. In our basic training there was the infiltration course, and, in a nighttime, you can see the bullets fly past your head. How dumb can a person be, kindly take a look at me. The traces of flying from the M-16 machine gun and like a fool I raise my head up high just to watch the traces going by. My helmet flew off of my head and therefore I had to fall on my stomach back to get my helmet. The soldiers are saying to me you are going the wrong way stupid, but I still had to go get my helmet.

I finally got my helmet and put it back on my head. Dan like everyone else I called on my stomach, of course the infiltration course. The sergeant said to me what county idiot will turn around and call the other way, I didn't even know what the hell to say. The other Sgt. started tapping him on his shoulder, and then told him look at his head. The sergeant said you damn dummy you raise your head; don't you even know the helmet was shut off your head. He took the helmet off my head, and there was a straight line across the helmet. In the sergeant told me this is why he flew off of your head. Being young and dumb it matters not what age, it is how you are able to stand up and walk away. I am one veteran who can perform KP, this is called kitchen duties. You do not have to ask me to wash the dishes that are dirty, nor clean the floors.

I ironed all the clothes of my house and that includes my wife's clothing and my daughter's clothing. I can fix and repair cause, in case I am delayed. The problems that we have which lead up to suicide, is not the knowledge nor understanding of what could be in your way. Before I went into the service both my feet were crushed and Uncle Sam still, I love being to serve my country. I am a psychiatrist I am a doctor I am a therapist I am a social worker I am here for you. There's nothing a veteran cannot learn, nor is there any job in which we cannot do. I know on my medicine this too much; I know how to have it cut down; by telling the person the problem happened because of the medication. This is a problem that many veterans do not understand, nor do they not understand why it is that their family; do not understand what they are going through. I was told was your family in Vietnam which you, now you know why Dale think like you. Do you think I'm not a doctor, I can tell you how many times my two big tolls; they want to cut them off. I tell my wife Anna tell my daughter, never let that happen. Being the doctor that I am I know and understand that they will be cut off one day in the future to come. My grandmother and hundreds of other veterans. Have had this done to them and next comes the ankle then the entire leg.

I have seen it done too many times, understanding and understanding what I just said to you is why I am a doctor. From the battlefield of many who one known and unknown gone this understanding is real. I feel the pain from the toe, and I feel Howard it grows. The decision that I make other decisions that you have to make, it is the energy of the wounded warrior that he or she must understand, what is the best way to walk throughout this land. I am not the only one living in pain, I see this each and every day. Five times I tried suicide, for some reason he says you're not going anywhere; you work for me. Veterans and civilians of all living in hell. You must open that mouth, then let it out. You may think life is great, I for one love every part of it. Life's challenges are always on the front line, it is what you do when you get there.
When you think you cannot do nothing, to change the way that you are living; you are wrong we call it one day at a time. I pray each

and every day, and the words that I say. Thank
you, father, for this day and everything in it. I
sat on top of tops and in my mind, I said jump
or don't jump. I am not in charge of father in
heaven is in charge, he is not just our father in
heaven is everywhere. I took the time to talk to
you and hope for some reason that I get
through. I for one cannot get angry or sad or
mad! Yes, I am a scorpion and the poison I
can give to you. Is something that I don't want
to do, because my father in heaven is the one
that's walking me through.

I am not the only one who has been to hell, but
all the others will not tell. By them keeping it in,
this sometimes brings you to the end. If you
think this suicide stops the wrong, listen to the
worth some trying to tell you; understand the
words that I say. This is how you can live for
another day! No one said it would be easy,
and there is no one there to count your tears.
Don't you know you will forever have those
fears, that for some reason when not
disappear. The energy for wounded warriors,
therefore you have the strength to live for
another day. One day at a time of some of the
words that they say, these words can also help
you to live for another day. Have faith in God
as I do, he will help you get through. There's a
whole lot of things that I could say, most of you
when not understand any way.

I keep wondering of all the things I would like to do, why do I still feel like a fool. My financing is bad if I had a higher score, I will be glad. I am the one who has to make that change, the more ways than one I will get this job done! Veteran or civilian you must learn to stand tall, he will be there to get you through it all. Have faith in thyself, don't be the one who always yell; that's the one who will land in hell. Educate yourself and a better way to live. The is not easy especially the way I feel, tomorrow's another day; get up and walk away. You can get through it understand what I say, energy for the wounded warrior; get the hell up and walk away!

Pain Don't Give Up!

We have come together at one time or another and have compared our thoughts for what it may be worth. Life itself can bring your fortune and fame or a darkness deeper than you can think. Has anyone ever come forth to you, and spoke about the ups and downs in their life; a what a pain one person can be towards another? Have you sat on a park bench and said to yourself why in the hell I might going through this? This can have the meanings of living in visible life, due to the facts that you feel you are the guilty one;

unfortunately, the fingers always pointed toward you. What is it that you want to do, other programs that are in your head; programs of the future still to come? Have you been taught to think positively, and yet you feel your life is in a negativity form? Step forward and admit to all the pains, in which you feel each day in your life. The word pain significantly to the point, forces fears plus unthinkable modes that change in your life. Pain can estimate how you breathe in your life and the other significantly ways that Sorrels into and to your life. Have talked about both of my feet being crushed, somewhere in the affinities of the age of 12 years old.

I had the age of 70 years old at this time and date County do the math of how many years I walked this earth in pain. For one moment can you take one second and think of how many others for any reasons. Which can enter into your mind and you may think of others and pain more years than I have lived in pain. A human being living in pain, constantly may think it is not necessary; for you to know that this the type of life in which they live. Their way of thinking is how sorry you will feel for them and that is the last thing or feelings that they want to know. One thing about the pains in life, is the point of which you come to; that you have found a better way. I myself am blessed to still be alive, thinking of all the relatives that I know; that are no longer here with me. My father in heaven is home I love; he has always been there; with the love in which he shares. What enters into your mind can also change your blood pressure and at the same time alter the way that you think. Happy one moment and said the next moment. You cannot control in any way, how you can live each and every day. The one thing about pain, there are many levels that it can show up. What can you possibly do about the pains of life, you can adjust yourself; into a better way of thinking? Stop for one moment and understand what I say.

Even though my feet my hurt on the treadmill I will walk, for more than an hour and a half. Whatever hurts me I will find a better way, to extend that pain in another way. The body pains sometime will not go away, therefore the medicine shows up at your door; and sometimes you end up at the store. The worst of the things that can happen in your life, you the one who have to sacrifice. One must be honest with thyself and take those brains of yours up off of that shelf. There are times when you lose someone who has been close throughout your life, somehow in that period of time you must ask our father in heaven to help you through this time. Unfortunately, pain is never easy and sometimes and never goes away. You must be don't want to stand up tall and as I always say get through it all. When I add of the years of all of my sacrifice, I only wish my true love was full of spice. Each and every day things don't have to go your way, you're the one who was to stand up and get the hell back out there plus pray. The pains that comes in so many ways, the hard to figure out in so many ways. When there's someone who you trust as someone who you love. Lots of times this is the way, that you can go out with a smile on your face. You know I can do this alone, have confidence and a friend of yours who will help you do it all. To tell you the truth what others will not say, I can tell you all the times that I cried for a better way.

 I said to myself how could I be so wrong, when others you love now you don't get along. Down on my knees I remember how I prayed; heavenly father kindly shows me the right way. What makes you think that you're the one, that's a problem you have had all along. Still pointing the fingers at thyself, is why your brains of steel on that shelf. Yes, you can love someone with all your heart, the next thing you know you live in a part. Your heart is broken with not one damn good word to say, on the other side of that door is where you have to stay. You cannot satisfy everyone in any shape or form, take my word for it you soon be outside the same door. How do you feel about the things in your life, other good or bad are you willing to sacrifice? When the tears come down as a reasoning as they say, don't look at the destiny it is over as they say. County don't understand the words that I say, because many of you can give a damn anyway. But if your heart is broken and you are feeling the same pain. Say a blessing and get the hell out of the way. I'm happy for all who were in love and life is the best of ways. Family stay together what do blessing as I say. For those who pay the course to be the boss, this is one will say; whatever you do understand that your life which can change. If the possibility of working out things once the problem is understood, hold each other's hands and look into your eyes I'm sure you will both survive. Love is long but life is short for eternity around life is short and love as long.

In which way in life the you now live for the best, I hope. Pain don't give up and the only true meaning of this, is a better way to live. One can always say I'm sorry and make a better day, this will never work for those who love to go out and play. A true blessing comes from far above, this is what happened when I fell in love. Today there is no fear solely because, there is no love around here. If I can put my arms around you, and just for one moment hold you tight. The tears will come down my face, plus my heart will be back in grace. Of course, I am the one to blame and I'm hoping this will make you feel great. But deep in my heart, my thinking is my mistakes. This is not the first time that I've lived in pain, I've had to learn to give myself a break. I thank you for the blessing of the times that we shared, and I've got the message that I am out of here. Truthfully, I must think and find a better way, to hold my head high as I say goodbye. If you are one who is feeling the pain, don't give up just walk away! You will make it and some will be on your way! Thanks to my father in heaven, many of us will live for another day. Sometimes you'll sacrifice in order to have a good life, make sure it's understood, by you that life will be good. One day at a time this is what many say, the God our father blessings you like me will be on our way!

Never Forget True Love!

From the numbers 1 to 10 can you tell me; how many times have you told someone you love them. From the numbers 1 to 10, how many times a day tell you they love you? For the numbers 1 to 10, from this day is it true or false. Never forget true love, can be a blessing in more ways than one? Good and bad true and false in and out up and down. Facts nonfiction reality reservation motivation real-life infatuation. Can you imagine the mood that you are in, when there's a smile on your face? Do you remember when the thought of those in your pass, put a smile on your face. It was the thought of a dinner date, soon to come that I cannot wait for. Never forget that love, whether they are near or far. Are you one home has had family at a far distance, then you had ever wanted them to be. Which your communications with them, only wishing you can come together this day. Have you cry like a baby, for those that you still miss and wish you can help them tightly, for the love that you still miss? It is not always your fault, nor will things always go your way. B yet you were here thinking, you all come together one day. I remember when I came home alone, all by myself from Vietnam.

My mother was in my mind, every day in my life. My mother who brought me back to life, but all those terrible thoughts I came home with each night. It could be a better way for me to live this day, but that my mother there would be no life for me to display. Never forget true love, no matter which day, my mother's life keeps me alive each day. The most impossible thing that a person can say, is how you miss your family that are far far away. Many of you are separated in different ways and having your mind how you miss your family in certain ways. Listen to what I'm saying family keep someone in your heart, this will always make you feel better to get to that day. Of course, we still have those ups and those downs, no matter what happens you will still have to move around. There have been times when I said to a loved one, have a nice day. I stop saying to the how much I love them, to them it was just a game. I told him how much I missed them and how much I love them with all my heart. Even as they get older, they find many ways to stay or part. Now is their children's children's home I like to see this day, not just on Facebook; but knocking at my door one day? Yes, I'm the old the one and they are the younger ones on their way. I would love to hear them say grandpa, kindly come out let's play. You can never be lonely, with love deep in your heart; when you think of a loved one forever and your heart. Don't blame anyone for your ups and downs, he did love in your mind like I do all the time. My future is my hope of the family far away, that we will get together and have fun one day. Christina keeps my blood flowing, and things that I have to do.

 Just like my mother my baby girls love is true. Yes, is true I do speak of many others, no matter what their names may be. I am the oldest and sometimes of my age I can get away. I have called to many others and said how much I love them. I'm hoping they understand that my love is throughout the land. The Christina J. Is always near and shares her love with me throughout the entire year. Not taking anything from any other, is her love they keep me stronger. Weather is one love to love or even eight who you love. Just knowing they love you, will give you the strength from high above. Not to say anything good or bad about anybody throughout this land. But which is the love that you understand, that'll make you smile plus walk throughout the land. I love all my family members; this I hope they understand. But one of the best things that can happen, is a love that is close at hand. Sometimes my mind thinks terrible thoughts, of this life I have at hand. Only to think of Christina and the life we have at hand. How many times can you say to someone that you love them, for some reason you think they don't understand. All because the wood others may have told them, that makes them think of you, as a friend they would not stand. Details this told of how you bold and did not take any bull from anyone they were told. I serve my country and to this day I stand tall, and less than 1.3 seconds I will get into a brawl. The thought of me loving someone and have them understand.

Is one of the reasons Christina J Williams health me walk this land. I compare my mother and the love she always gave. The Christina J Williams the love is still the same way! Pick somebody in your thoughts I remember the words I'm saying. With that love and all of its power, you can live with the reason for everything to be true. Just to know that someone out there who loves you! My heart has been broken in more ways than one and I remember to this day life is no fun. I don't know why I'm still alive, one thing I know there's never any surprise; a wish stays out of here or which day I will be there I never had time to think my day was near. For one who is I am, with no fear of the end; without the love she shared I will not even be here. Have you ever feared of being alone I've been that way many a day, and then it was the love that I thought of each day?   Have you ever said I love you to someone, and they still act like they don't understand? This does happen to someone and others have no love. Never forget true love, to those who love to share; and a lot of times in life they do not have to be near. Make my day is with some will say, only if life is to live, if the love of your heart is from within.

I truly miss my mother, as well is many others; not one has ever said I love you in any way? You cannot make someone say I love you, not coming from the heart if they meet it from the start. When I first met you, I fell in love with you, and said those words each day. No matter what the reasons I can tell you for sure, always like this will never again come your way! We do give a damn if I want to the land, if I don't, I'm sure you get paid; to say yes, I did love him in one of two ways. If there's someone that you truly love, take the time and let them know. If you don't do this, you might be buried deep and below. Never forget true love no matter what their names, and never forget the smiles they put on your face. I love you family in every way, but for some reason those were to never say! I've taken the time to tell you each and every day, it seems to me like those words went the other way. I say once again before is the end, families I love you in many ways and don'ts around me in the end with tears making others think you cared! If you love someone tell them now, not when the times that'll make you frown! Never forget true love, when true love is near.   Thank You Ma- Ma and Christina J. Williams For Being Near!!!

www.ingramcontent.com/pod-product-compliance
Lightning Source LLC
Chambersburg PA
CBHW071415290426
44108CB00014B/1839